HO
EAT WE
ON A
WHEAT, GLUTEN
AND DAIRY FREE DIET

A Survival Guide
by
Fran Crosthwaite

©Copyright Fran Crosthwaite 1997, 2000, 2001, 2004
2006

ISBN 1 872560 15 6

1998 First published by Merton Books
2000, 2001, 2004 Updated and published by Merton Books
2006 Fifth updated edition published by Merton Books
Sponsored by YorkTest Laboratories

MERTON BOOKS

PO Box 279, Twickenham, Middlesex TW1 4XQ
Tel: 0208 892 4949 Fax: 0208 892 4950
e-mail: merton.books@btinternet.com
www.mertonbooks.co.uk

INTRODUCTION

As you are reading this booklet you presumably have, or suspect that you have, food intolerance; but do not give up hope – you most certainly can eat well! Over the last ten years more and more alternative foods and ingredients have become available and many are easily accessible from supermarkets. Food labelling has dramatically improved and you will now regularly see specific notes such as 'Gluten Free' and 'May contain traces of nuts'. This is much to our advantage as food intolerance sufferers, as it not only makes our lives easier, it also increases the range of foods that we can safely buy. Most supermarkets seem to have separate sections now for 'special diet' foods, with names like "Freefrom" or "Freedom", and this really does make shopping much quicker as you can go straight to a wide selection of 'permitted' food items, instead of having to search through whole isles full! A word of caution though – do still check the ingredients lists just in case something YOU cannot tolerate is included. The organic ranges are also very good, being very clearly labelled. They tend not to have so many 'added' ingredients, so are well worth checking out. Many of the ready-made sauces are gluten and wheat free, and some are also dairy free. So in most supermarkets you will find a good range of basic foods from milk and butter alternatives, bread mixes, biscuits, cereals and pastas to fresh foods such as ready baked loaves and gluten-free sausages.

Extremely good substitutes are now available for most foods, but bread still remains a bit of a problem. Although you can now buy bread mixes and loaves quite easily they are often very crumbly in texture and taste better toasted. Do try as many as you can, to find one that suits you and your life style. (*See also Breadmaker recipe.)* The lists of commercially branded foods included here are not all that is available as more foods are being introduced all the time, but use them as a starting point to shop effectively for foods that meet your own dietary needs.

Even when using the lists you still need to read labels with care, looking for any suspect items. Never assume anything and if in doubt do ask. All supermarkets now have lists of the ingredients in their own products, so at the bakery or deli counters they can check for you. Some supermarkets will supply you with lists or booklets on request or have helpful information on their websites.

You will certainly see plenty of GLUTEN FREE foods, but do take care with these as many contain WHEAT STARCH, which is perfectly acceptable for coeliacs but not for those with wheat intolerance. There are occasions when you should ask for a label check if you are unable to do it for yourself: for example, if you are staying in a hotel or eating out in a restaurant. Although the chef should be aware of coeliac requirements he may not realise that gluten free rolls are not suitable for your diet. A quick look at the ingredients label will ensure that you enjoy your holiday or meal out without any subsequent reaction.

Do be careful with flavoured crisps too. Wheat is used so that the flavouring flows freely when added to the crisps, but was not always included in the labelling. Hopefully with the stricter labelling codes this will now be noted!

Do try not to rely too heavily on any single food. Even those who are severely restricted in foods they can tolerate should aim to have as varied a diet as possible, trying out some alternatives. There is now such a good choice readily available this should not prove too difficult. For example you can substitute dairy products with soya milk and spreads as well as ice-cream and yoghurts, or you can introduce rice milk, goats' cheese and goats' milk, so that you are not relying on only one product. As your new diet may be for life it is best to make it as interesting as you possibly can.

You will need to try alternative ingredients, and the key to this is to experiment! If something does not work try a different variation. As you become more familiar with the different ingredients you will soon learn which work well in one recipe but not in another. Do not be discouraged by failure but look on it as a learning process and try again. It is often a good idea to make a note of what you have done so that you can repeat it if the result was satisfactory, or modify it if the result was disappointing.

Another important aspect of a wheat and gluten free diet is the loss of a number of good sources of dietary fibre. You must make every effort to include large amounts of fresh fruit and vegetables into your new diet, and many of these raw. Pulses are a good source of fibre, so do try out all the different varieties now available in both health food shops and supermarkets. You will find them very useful carbohydrate food and, added to a soup for example, they make a complete and satisfying meal.

If you have neither the time nor the inclination to experiment for yourself, it is still possible to enjoy a varied diet. You should find you are able to buy many suitable products from either your local supermarket or a good health food shop. If you cannot find what you want keep asking – it's the only way to increase awareness and keep the supermarkets and health food shops on their toes! You can now get a soya milk coffee in Starbucks and whilst visiting the Eden Project recently I discovered that I could have purchased a fresh gluten-free sandwich in one of the restaurants! This really does indicate a huge step forward for all us food intolerance sufferers, and show that we really can eat well again!

Fran Crosthwaite

USEFUL CONTACTS

Call these numbers, ask for Customer Services, state the 'free from' own label lists you need and they will be mailed to you.

Asda :	0500 1000 55
Boots:	08450 70 80 90
Co-op :	0800 0686 727
Marks & Spencer :	0845 302 1234
Safeway/Morrisons :	0845 611 6111
Sainsbury :	0800 63 62 62
Somerfield & Kwiksave :	0117 935 6669
Tesco :	0800 505 555
Waitrose :	0800 188884

They all have information on websites, though do not always display the lists of 'free from' foods which are stocked in store.

www.asda.co.uk
www.safeway.co.uk
www.sainsburys.co.uk (no lists)
www.co-op.co.uk
www.boots.com
www2.marksandspencer.com
www.somerfield.co.uk
www.tesco.com

FORBIDDEN FOODS

Dairy Foods

Buttermilk
Biscuits, cakes and some breads
Caseinates and casein
Cheese
Chocolate
Dried skimmed mild powder
Evaporated and tinned milk
Ice cream
Lactalbumin
Milk, cream, butter, margarine
Non-fat milk solids
Whey and whey powder
Yoghurt and yoghurt drinks

Wheat and Gluten

Any food in a breadcrumb or batter coating e.g. fish fingers
Any food containing rusk, e.g. sausages or beefburgers
Any food on a pastry or biscuit crumb base
Baking powder
Biscuits
Bread in any shape or form
Bulger wheat
Cakes and pastries
Crackers
Crisps (flavoured)
Cous Cous
English mustard

Wheat and Gluten *(continued)*

Fast food restaurant chips - they are often coated in flour to crisp them up more rapidly

Gravy cubes, granules and powders

Hydrolysed Vegetable Proteins (HVP) (unless made with Soya)

Ice creams with wafers

Instant sauces and casserole mixes

Liquorice

Monosodium Glutomate

Pasta and noodles

Pâtés

Peanuts (dry-roasted)

Pickles, sauces, salad creams and mayonnaise

Pizza

Sandwich fillings and spreads

Semolina

Snack foods for children - read labels with care

Soya sauce

Starch, modified starch, wheat starch, edible starch

Stock cubes *(see list for safe commercial products)*

Stuffing

Suet

Sweets and chocolates with biscuit or wafer content

Tinned and packet soups

Tinned meat products

Tinned pie fillings

Vacuum packed and frozen ready meals *(See list for safe commercial products)*

Wheat or whole-wheat cereals, or those containing wheat, rye, barley or oats

ALTERNATIVE AND SAFE FOODS

Dairy

Carob confectionery

Creamed coconut and nut creams

Goat or sheep milk products (milk, cheese and yoghurt) can be tolerated by some people

Soya yoghurts and desserts

Rice milk

Soya milk, margarines, cream and ice creams, and "cheeses"

Sunflower and vegetable margarines

Soya baby milk formulas

Tofu both firm and soft

Tofu cheeses

Nut butter and spreads

White Flora

Wheat and Gluten

All fresh vegetables, meat and fish

All types of fruit, tinned foods in brine, oil or natural juice, e.g sardines, peaches etc.

All pulses such as lentils, peas, chickpeas, kidney beans etc.

Arrowroot flour

Buckwheat groats, flour and flakes, pasta

Carob powder

Chestnut flour, banana flour and yam flour

Cornflakes, rice krispies, puffed rice

Gram flour (chickpeas)

Wheat and Gluten
(continued)

Jellies

Maize meal, organic cornflour, some cornflour, corn pasta

Millet flakes and flour

Nuts and dried fruit

Popping corn

Potatoes and potato starch or flour

Polenta

Quinoa grain and flour

Rice and rice flour, wild rice, rice flakes, rice noodles

Rice cakes, but read labels carefully as some do contain wheat or rye

Sago grains and flour

Soya beans – flour, flakes and bran

Spelt flour (can be tolerated by some so try it and see for yourself)

Sweet potatoes

Tapioca grains and flour

SAFE BRANDED FOODS

Special note

D/F = Dairy Free. Foods marked (NOT D/F) contain some milk product, but no wheat or gluten.

Do remember that manufacturers change ingredients from time to time. This means that even the foods on the following lists will need a label check just to be sure. Any HVP used has been checked and is soya based, and therefore safe.

Reference to "Own brand" are foods produced under the label of a particular supermarket or store.

Baking Powders

Cantassium salt free baking powder

Sainsbury baking powder

Bread, Flour Mixes, Crackers and Plain Biscuits

Biona Pumpernickell and Organic Wholemeal Rye breads (not strictly gluten free but tolerated by some so try for yourself and see)

Bioculinar gluten and wheat free baking mix, brown and white

Clear Spring sesame wafers (rice cakes)

Dietary Specialities Bread mix, Pizza mix, chocolate fudge cake mix, sponge cake mix, Brownie mix, Flour mix, also biscuits and crackers

Doves Farm speciality flours, gluten free white and brown, rice flour and gram flour and white and brown bread flour

Dr Karg seeded Spelt Crackers

EnerG white and brown rice bread, tapioca bread

Glutano biscuits

Bread, Flour Mixes, Crackers and Plain Biscuits
(continued)

Granny Ann Premier biscuits

Health Choice organic rice cakes

Kallo rice cakes, thick, thin sliced and snack size

Lima rice cakes with millet, or buckwheat

Nutricia Glutafin range of foods

Orgran corn crispbreads, also rice or millet, and organic rice thins, Pizza mix, self-raising flour, cake mixes and bread mixes, as well as porridge and museli mixes.

"Own brand" rice cakes

Pure Harvest millet rice cakes (distributed by Clear Spring)

Ryvita rice cakes

SnapBrand mini organic rice cakes with sesame and salt (snack size)

Stamp Collection organic and wheat free all-purpose flour and ready baked loaves

Sunnyvale mixed grain sourdough bread

Tesco gluten free cookies (not D/F)

Trufree flours, biscuits, Herb & onion crackers.

Village Bakery: some cakes/puddings and biscuits are suitable

Cereal

Some breakfast cereals contain malt, malt flavouring or malt extract. If you are on a VERY strict diet avoid those marked (*), as malt is made from barley, and go for the health shop varieties.

Kallo 100% organic puffed rice cereal – plain and honey coated

Kellogs: Cornflakes*, Frosties*, Crunchy Nut Flakes*, Rice Krispies*, Coco Pops* (not D/F)

Nature's Path Organic Mesa Sunrise flakes and Crispy Rice

Sainsbury: Cornflakes*, Honey nut cornflakes*, Rice Pops*, Coco Snaps* (not D/F)

Tesco: Cornflakes*, Crisp Puffed Rice*, Sugar Frosted Flakes* Coco Puffs* (not D/F)

Whole Earth organic cornflakes

Confectionery and Sweet Biscuits

The Carob Confectionery Co: CrispiBar, Dairyfree Carob Bar, and Full Cream Milk Carob Bar (W/F), Carob Beenys

Carob Hippo Drops

Castus Fruit Bar with sesame, with apricot

Elite sesame halva

Grizzly Bars – blackcurrant, pineapple and papaya, banana and pear, apricot and honey

Hollymill Pressed Fruit Bars: Oat Cereal Bars – lemon, raspberry, apple and cardamom, hazelnut, apricot and almond

Carriba Dairyfree and two W/F varieties

Kallo Apple & cinnamon and Caramel (not D/F) mini rice cakes

La Fama Spanish Turron

Lazzaroni Amaretti di Saronno

Merba Almond Macaroons

Plamil mint chocolate with soya and plain chocolate with soya and roasted hazelnuts

Sainsbury Fruity Crisp and Corn Crisp (not D/F)

Confectionery and Sweet Biscuits
(continued)

Shepherds Boy Fruit and Nut Bar with Sunflowers and New Organic Shepherds Boy Fruit and Nut Bars: coconut, apple, banana, ginger, multifruit

Snackajacks – chocolate flavour

SuperCook Decorating Marzipan in three natural colours and Whisk and Bake Meringue

Telma Halva – vanilla flavour

Tesco Meringue Nests and Snowballs (not D/F)

Also: Sesame seed bars

Instant Potato

Mr Mash Instant Potato

Smash

Yeoman Instant Mashed Potato

Margarine

Granose Sunflower, Vegetable, Soya margarines

Meridian soya margarine

Pure soya, sunflower and organic

Sainsbury soya and soya half fat spread, dairy free, vegetable margarine

Suma sunflower

Tomor block dairy free margarine

Vitaquell

SAFE BRANDED FOODS

Milks, Yoghurts, Desserts, Ice Creams

Alpro soya milks – chocolate and plain, yoghurts plain and flavoured, and dairyfree desserts in chocolate, vanilla, caramel and forest fruits.

Bio Organic Rice and Rice Dessert in Cacao and Vanilla

Cedaridge Sheeps' milk yoghurt

Cedaridge goats' milk yoghurt

Goatherd UHT goats' milk

Granose soya milk, organic soya milk and sugar free soya milk and soya yoghurt

Holland & Barrett natural goats' milk yoghurt and sugar and salt free soya milk, plain soya milk

Mill Milk – oat drink

Plamil soya milk rice pudding, and sugar free rice pudding with sultanas

Pertwood Farm Wild Organic Sticky Toffee Pudding, Fudge, Chocolate and Tangy Lemon Puddings.

Provamel soya milk

Rice Dream and *Lima Rice Drink* – original, vanilla and chocolate flavours

Sainsbury 'Freefrom' Just Pour dairy free alternative to single cream and 'Freefrom' ready made custard

Sainsbury lemon sorbet, the Real Ice Co. Mango sorbet

Sainsbury's Longlife soya milk, and calcium enriched with apple juice

So Good organic soya milk and yoghurts and Soyacreem

Sojasun – Organic Live Soya Yogurts plain and flavoured, Probiotic drink, and crème fraiche

Milks, Yoghurts, Desserts, Ice Creams
(*continued*)

Swedish Glace – non-dairy ice dessert in vanilla, chocolate, strawberry and raspberry and new 'chocolate' coated ice-cream on a stick - 'Smooth Vanilla'

Sunrise Goats' naturally frozen goats' milk ice cream

Sunrise non-dairy frozen desserts ice cream, Carob Ice and Tofutti Chocolate Cuties

Tesco soya milk, unsweetened, with sugar, calcium enriched with fruit sugar

Tregaron Foods spray dried goats' milk

Unisoy Gold Organic soya milk and soya yoghurt

Waitrose soya and rice milks

Woodland Park live goats' milk yoghurt and live sheeps' milk yoghurt

Pasta, Noodles and Grains

Apache BioTaco Shells

Blue Dragon rice noodles

Conimex Chinese Rice Noodles Mihun

De Boles Thin Spaghetti Substitute, Elbows, Shells (100% corn)

Direct Foods Quinoa

EnerG pasta

Galettes de Riz Rice Paper

Instant corn lasagne sheets and spaghetti

Kallo low fat polenta

La Veneziane 100% Corn Pasta

Mrs Lepper's Corn Spaghetti, Corn Elbows

Soba 100%Japanese Buckwheat Pasta, and King Soba Corn & Brown Rice Noodles

Orgran Wheat/gluten free pasta – Herb and spinach, Cracked pepper, 100% Buckwheat, rice and millet

Primavera Pasta, corn and spinach

Salute spaghetti, penne and pasta twists (from Asda and Sainsbury)

Trufree Lasagne

UK Grown Quinoa

Vitaspelt organic spelt elbows and spaghetti

Also - some flavoured packet rices are OK. Check labels

Pasta Sauces and Mayonnaise

Dolmio sauce for Pasta with Olives

Florentino concentrated Vegetarian Sauce Bolognese

Green Dragon 'NNAISE

Kite Wholefoods Mayonnaise

Meridian Mayo

Sacia Pâté di Olive

Santinis: Veronese, Marettino, Pomodoro, Siciliana

Whole Earth Italiano Spaghetti Sauce

Zest Foods – all pasta sauces, NOT Pesto Sauce. This is not D/F

SAFE BRANDED FOODS

Pâtés and Spreads

Bovril

Fromsoya with garlic and herbs

Marmite

Meridian Cashew Butter and Light Tahini

Natrex Yeast extract original savoury spread

Sunita Whole Tahini creamed sesame

Tartex Swiss Yeast Pâtés: all flavours

Urd Pâtés: Hazelnut, Mushroom, Provence

Vecon Original vegetable stock

Vegemite (contains malt extract)

Vessen: Herb, Red Pepper, Mushroom

Whole Earth Hummus Tahini

Also: Peanut butters, supermarket hommous

Sausages and Burgers

Asda Gluten free pork and onion sausages

BirdsEye Steak House All Beef Grillsteaks, 2 Prize Grills, and 100% Beefburgers

Marks & Spencer Top Quality Fresh Pork Sausages (Not D/F)

Sainsbury Taste the Difference Pork & Herb sausages

Tesco Freefrom Fresh Pork Sausages – Gluten free

Waitrose "Cambridge" Gluten free sausages

Also: Some Continental Sausages are suitable – check labels

SAFE BRANDED FOODS

Snack Foods

Bearitos Organic Blue corn chops – Tortilla and Organic Croustilles Tortila chips

Butterkist Butter Toffee popcorn (not D/F)

Corn Busters original sweetened popcorn

Cornnuts (toasted corn snack similar to nuts)

Country Harvest Bombay Mix Chevda

Golden Valley Poppop Microwave popcorn ready salted

Hoggits Snack organic corn

Holland & Barrett Bombay mix and Banana chips

Infinity Foods: Trail mix, Bombay mix, Chickpea mix, Spicy noodles

Kelp Crunchies Blue Cheese (not D/F)

Molen Aartje Corn Peanuts organic snack

OK bars – blueberry & cinnamon and apricot

Old El Paso Nacho Chips, taco shells and mini taco shells

Orgran Fruit filled bars – various flavours

Sainsbury Bhajia Mix, Cornitos and Indonesian style crackers

Sharwoods Puppadoms, Indian Madras spiced puppadums and plain puppodums, and Prawn crackers

Tesco Bombay mix

Soups and Tinned Foods

Heinz: Baked Beans, Cream of Tomato Soup (not D/F)

Hera Soup Mixes: Lentil and Bacon, Thick Pea, Vegetable Goulash

Triangle Foods: Mushroom and Potato Soup, Leek and Potato Soup, Vegetable Soup

Spices and Seasonings

Schwartz curry powders, herb blends, microwave browning products, seasoned peppers, authentic curry blends

Sharwood Curry Paste: Hot, Mild, Tandori, Vindaloo

Home Gourmet range of seasoning mixes for Thai, Indonesian and Chinese dishes

Stock Cubes & Sauces

Free & Easy Cheese flavoured sauce mix and Vegetable Gravy sauce mix

Friggs stock cubes

Just Bouillion stocks

Infinity Foods Tamari sauce

Kallo vegetable stock cubes and vegetable stock powder

Lima Tamari soy sauce

Meridian Foods Tamari soya sauce

Orgran wheat and gluten free gravy mix

Also: Soya cubes

SAFE BRANDED FOODS

Suet

Ashland shredded vegetable suet

Broadlands vegetable suet rolled in rice flour

Tofu Products and Cheeses, Sheep and Goat Cheeses

Bute Island Foods: Scheese – soya based solid food in Cheshire or Mozzarella styles

Cauldron Foods Original Tofu, Naturally Smoked Tofu

Florentino Diaryfree vegetarian Parmazano

High Weald Sheep's cheeses

Kallo from soya "Soft Cheese"

Marigold Health Foods Tinned Braised Tofu

Mori-nu Tofu – Firm and Silken

Parait Products Tofu cheese

Redwood Co of London Tofu cheese – Cheatin' Cheddar Style Cheezly

SoHoSoft Savoury Cashew Spread – Plain and Garlic Herb

Soya Kaas Cheddar style "cheese"

Soymage low fat sour cream and cream cheese alternative

Tofutti cream "Cheese"

Wieldwood Farm Dairy Sheep FETA and Walda

Also: Fresh goats' cheeses available in supermarkets and some sheep's cheese

and user friendly. A great deal of useful information about these products is available on each website and they all offer more details and advice by contacting their customer service. Some provide lengthy product lists on line, but when you find that just one 'free from' ingredient can run into literally thousands of products, it is not surprising that most supermarkets prefer either to offer a selected list or invite you to ask for a full one to be sent to you. There are differences in how comprehensive and useful each group's list may be. It is worth getting to know the one that best suits your own particular needs.

Own label 'free from' foods from Asda are more comprehensive than most. They include products free from soya, shellfish, nuts, sesame seeds, cow's milk, wheat, yeast, egg, ozo colours, other additives and benzoate. They also stock Dove's Farm gluten free plain flour, as well as a number of Kallo products, Livewell products and Dietary Special mixes.

The Co-op has own label products suitable for wheat, gluten, milk and egg free diets.

Marks and Spencer do not have a separate area as yet for their 'free from' lines but carry a lot of information on their website including some 52 pages of product listing!

Somerfield's website offers a selection from their range of available 'free from' products - which includes 3312 which are egg-free!

There is a very large choice of gluten free products at Sainsbury's where they also stock other brands of foods such as Livewell, Orgran, Trufree and the Dietary Specials range, which includes a number of frozen foods such as pies, pizzas, lasagna etc, some of which are suitable. There are too many foods to list here, but visit the larger stores or their website and go to shop online, then search for items. Particularly helpful is their booklet *Product Guide for Nut Allergy Sufferers.*

The Tesco website gives you a good choice of gluten free products and they also have detailed nutritional information on low sugar, low sodium and low fats food lists which are available for the asking. They carry other brands such as Meridian Foods free from sauces, Orgran's range, and Dove's Farm flours. Again there are too many to list here, but look in store and you will be pleasantly surprised at the variety.

Waitrose own label range of products includes those suitable for milk/lactose free and gluten free diets. They too have quite a wide range of Orgran, Dietary Special and Livewell products in a designated 'free from' area. They also stock Stamp fresh bread and other varieties in the bread area. The Waitrose website is fabulously easy to use, and you can download a list of all the foods they stock which are suitable for you.

There are helpful lists, some not seen elsewhere, available from Boots, covering products free from celery, egg, fish, gluten, GMOs, maize, mayonnaise, milk, salt, sesame, soya, wheat and yeast. Most importantly they have lists of baby foods free from egg, soya and gluten.

If you prefer to shop locally, at a health food shop for example, then ask for the Orgran range which is very wide, as well as the Kallo range, the Dietary Specials range, the Livewell range and the Bakers Delight range. Dove's Farm do a big range of wheatfree flours too, and Trufree have a good choice of foods as well as "snack pots" which are often useful when travelling.

With so much on offer now, there is almost no excuse not to eat well!

See our USEFUL CONTACTS list on page 4 for quick reference to supermarket telephone numbers and website addresses

"CHEESY" PASTA

Quick lunch or supper dish for 4

1 quantity white sauce (see separate recipe) with a soya 'cheese' added to taste
8 oz/200g (uncooked weight) wheat free rice and garlic pasta shells, cooked as directed
4 rashers of streaky bacon, fried and chopped or 4 oz/100g Panacetta
Salt and pepper to taste
Extra 'cheese' to grate

Mix the hot cooked pasta, bacon and 'cheese' sauce together and place in a shallow oven-proof dish. Grate a little more soya 'cheese' over the top and put into the oven at Gas Mark 5, 375F or 190C until bubbling and lightly browned. Serve with a green salad, and Heinz baked beans.

BUCKWHEAT SALAD

A filling salad for 2
or serves 4 as a starter

3oz/85g buckwheat grains/groats
3oz tinned chickpeas
1 leek, washed, trimmed, sliced
2 large carrots, grated
2 hard-boiled eggs, quartered
2 tomatoes, chopped
Pinch of basil
Pinch of thyme
Sunflower oil for frying

Put the buckwheat into a bowl and cover with boiling water. Leave to stand, so that the buckwheat fluffs up. (If this does not happen put the buckwheat and water into a saucepan and gently bring to the boil again, then leave to stand.) Drain the buckwheat. Heat the oil in a pan and sauté the leek. Add the herbs, and then the buckwheat and continue to sauté to remove any excess water. Put this mixture into a serving dish and add the drained chickpeas, grated carrots, chopped nuts and egg.

Prepare a dressing as follows:

3 tablespoons olive oil
1-2 tablespoons lemon juice
Salt and pepper to taste
1 tablespoon fresh chopped mint
2 tablespoons fresh chopped parsley

Beat the lemon juice into the oil and then add the rest of the ingredients, seasoning to taste. Pour over the buckwheat salad and serve with salad leaves and cucumber.

SAUSAGEMEAT

Try this as a sausagemeat pie for a family supper
Serves 4

4oz/100g buckwheat flakes
8oz/200g minced pork (it does need to be quite fatty)
1 small onion, finely chopped
1 teaspoon mixed herbs
Salt and pepper

Put the buckwheat flakes into a bowl and just cover with boiling water. Leave to stand for a few minutes and then stir well. The mixture should become thick and sticky. Add the rest of the ingredients and mix very well. Use in any recipe that requires sausagemeat, or make into sausage shapes and fry gently.

WHITE SAUCE

This basic recipe can be used for both savoury and sweet sauces

2oz/50g dairy free margarine
2 tablespoons cornflour
½ pint soya milk
1 large egg, well beaten
salt and pepper

Melt the margarine and add the flour, stirring well. Add a little of the liquid to form a smooth paste. Remove from the heat and gradually add the rest of the liquid, stirring all the time to avoid lumps forming. Return the pan to the heat and cook for about 2 minutes or until the sauce is thick and smooth, stirring all the time. Remove from the heat again, allow to cool for a few minutes, and then add the well beaten egg. Return to the heat and bring to the boil again, stirring. Add seasoning to taste.

PASTRY

3oz/85g rice flour
2oz/50g potato flour
1oz/30g Gramflour (chickpea flour)
3oz/85g hard margarine or Tomor Dairy free fat
1 egg (beaten)
Pinch of salt

Sift the flours into a bowl and add a pinch of salt. Rub in the fat until the mixture resembles breadcrumbs, and then mix in the beaten egg until the mixture comes together to form a sticky ball. Using a well potato-floured surface roll out and use to line a dish or tin. At this point the pastry can be frozen and then filled and cooked from frozen. Otherwise fill and bake in the centre of the oven as required by the recipe. If the pastry is too dry and will not come together add a little water. If it is too sticky and will not roll out add more potato flour and shape into a ball. Cover with clingfilm and leave in the fridge for about 10-15 minutes. Do not leave it for too long as it will dry out and become unworkable.

Bake at Gas Mark 5, or 375F/190C.

To make a sweet pastry just add a dessert spoon of castor sugar to the flours and continue as above.

To cook a pie will take about 25 minutes, a flan 20 minutes and individual tarts about 15 minutes depending on your oven.

BACON AND LEEK QUICHE

A tasty family lunch or supper dish
Serves 4

1 quantity of pastry (see separate recipe)
1 quantity of white sauce (see separate recipe), but do not add the egg
2 eggs (size 3)
2 oz/50g streaky bacon, chopped and fried until crisp
1 trimmed, washed and chopped leek
Salt and pepper

Make up the pastry as directed and use to line a large shallow dish. Fill with ceramic beans and bake blind for about 10 minutes. Meanwhile make up the white sauce and then beat in two eggs. Add the bacon and leek, season to taste and pour the mixture into the prepared pastry case. Bake again for about 15 minutes, or until the filling is set and lightly browned. Serve warm or cold with a green salad.

Cook at Gas Mark 5, 375F/190C.

TUNA AND PASTA BAKE

A quick and easy dish to share
Serves 4

1 standard tin Heinz Tomato Soup or 1 x 14oz/400g tin chopped tomatoes
1 x 14oz/400g tin tuna flakes
1 clove garlic, crushed
Fresh or dried basil
4oz/100g (dry weight) Salute w/f Penne Quills (or any other w/f penne pasta)
Salt and pepper

Put the soup or tomatoes into an oven-proof dish and mix well with the tuna, garlic and basil. Next add the cooked pasta and stir well. Season to taste and cook in a preheated oven at Gas 4, 350F/180C, for about 20 minutes, or until piping hot and slightly brown on top. Serve with a green salad.

PANCAKES

Makes approx 8 pancakes

Use these as a dessert treat, or with a savoury filling of cooked rice, tuna and sweetcorn. Serve like cannelloni, with a savoury white sauce over them.

4oz/100g potato flour
2oz/50g Gram (chickpea) flour
1 egg (size 3)
5fl.oz water

continued over

PANCAKES continued

Sift the flours into a bowl and add the egg and half the water. Beat well to a smooth batter. Gradually add the rest of the water, beating all the time, until the mixture resembles thin cream. If making savoury pancakes season the mixture with salt and pepper.

Heat a heavy based pan until hot, and away from the heat add a little of the mixture, swirling the pan to ensure that it is evenly coated. The pan should be hot enough for the mixture to almost cook. Return to the heat for a few minutes and then turn the pancake over and cook on the other side for a few minutes.

Serve immediately with the lemon juice and sugar, or fill with a savoury mixture, roll up and keep warm, whilst cooking the rest of the mixture.

If the pancakes are too thick add more water to the mixture. The mixture must be thin enough to swirl around the pan and so cook almost immediately.

SPONGE CAKE

3oz/85g potato flour
2oz/50g gram (Chickpea) flour
1 heaped teaspoon w/f baking powder
2 medium eggs
3oz/95g soft margarine or soya fat
4oz/100g sugar
Flavouring such as vanilla essence, coffee, carob or chocolate, orange or lemon zest and juice

Cook at Gas Mark 4, 350F/180C on the middle shelf until light and springy to the touch.

Grease and line two 7″ baking tins.

Sift together the flours and baking powder into a large bowl. Add the other ingredients and mix well with a wooden spoon or electric whisk until the mixture is a pale yellow and a soft, slightly runny consistency. Spoon into the prepared tins, dividing evenly and smooth over.

Cook on the middle shelf until golden brown, about 25 minutes depending on your oven. Leave to cool for about 5 minutes and then remove from the tins and cool completely on a wire rack.

Sandwich them together with a filling of jam or lemon curd, or make soya fat "butter" cream and use that. This sponge is best eaten on the same day but will keep in an airtight tin for a day or two.

The recipe can also be used to make fruit sponge puddings or "Spotted Dick" and combined with almonds to make the filling for a Bakewell Tart.

YEAST BREAD

5oz/140g potato flour
4oz/100g organic cornflour
4oz/100g brown rice flour
1oz/30g Gram (chickpea) flour
1oz/30g buckwheat flour
2 level teaspoons of instant yeast granules
1 teaspoon salt
1 tablespoon vegetable or olive oil
12 fl ozs warm water
Cook at Gas Mark 5, 375F/190C in a greased and floured 1 lb loaf tin.

Sift the flours into a bowl with the instant yeast and the salt. Add the oil and then half the water. Mix well and gradually add the rest of the water until the mixture resembles a thick batter. Pour into the prepared tin and leave in a warm place until double in size. Place into a preheated oven, near the top, and cook for about 30 minutes. The bread is cooked when it starts to shrink away from the sides of the tin. Remove from the tin, and if you want a crusty loaf put back into the oven for about 8 minutes, or until the outside of the loaf is crisp and hard. Cool on a wire rack, and when completely cold slice and freeze, and use as required.

NUT MOCK CREAM

4oz/100g raw cashew nuts
2oz/50g creamed coconut
Approx 6 tablespoons water
A little honey to taste

Put all the ingredients into a blender or food processor and blend until smooth. If you don't have a blender, chop the nuts finely, beat all ingredients well together with a wooden spoon. Keep refrigerated.

SALMON WITH CREAMY DILL SAUCE

Serves 2

2 salmon fillets
1 leek, washed and thinly sliced
1 carton (250mls) of soya cream
1 teaspoon dried dill or tablespoon of fresh if available
Salt and pepper to taste
Oil for frying

Heat the oil in a heavy based frying pan, and gently fry the leek. Meanwhile grill the salmon fillets under a medium heat, turning after about 10 minutes. When the leeks begin to soften add the soya cream, dill, and season to taste. Allow to cook gently until the salmon is ready. Place the fillets onto the serving plates, and cover with the creamy leek and dill sauce. Serve with boiled new potatoes and green beans.

BEEF STROGANOV

Serves 4

1 medium onion, peeled and sliced
6oz/170g beef steak, cut into thin ribbons
Teaspoon of paprika
4 ozs mushrooms, washed and sliced thinly
1 carton (250mls) soya cream
Salt and pepper
Oil for frying

Heat the oil in a heavy based frying pan and add the onion, cooking for a few minutes, until transparent. Add the beef steak and paprika and brown quickly, before adding the mushrooms and soya cream. Stir gently and allow to simmer for a few minutes, until the beef is cooked and the sauce has turned brown. Season to taste with the salt and pepper, and serve with boiled rice and green salad.

MINESTRONE SOUP

Serves 4 to 6

4 large ripe tomatoes, peeled and chopped
1 large onion, peeled and chopped
2 cloves of garlic, peeled and crushed
1 teaspoon dried basil
¼ cabbage washed and shredded
2 courgettes, washed and finely chopped
1 tin haricot beans, drained and rinsed
2oz/50g w/f penne pasta or twists
1 tablespoon vegetable bullion
Salt and pepper
Olive oil
Water

Heat the oil in a large heavy based pan, and fry the onion until transparent. Add all the other vegetables and allow to sweat in the pan, covered for a few minutes. Add the rest of the ingredients, and cover with water. Bring up to the boil, and then simmer for about 20 minutes, stirring from time to time, or until the pasta and vegetables are cooked. This is a meal in itself!

You can vary the vegetables to what ever you have to hand, but always add tomatoes or tomato puree for a more authentic flavour!

MICROWAVE PORRIDGE

A quick but nutritious start to the day

To one packet of rice flakes (150g) add approx 75g weight each of millet flakes, quinoa flakes and buckwheat flakes. You can either add all three or those that you have to hand. You need at least two types of flakes to make an interesting porridge. Mix the flakes together well and store in an airtight container.

To make a bowl of porridge put three or four dessert spoons into a microwave-proof bowl, cover with water and microwave on full power for two minutes. Stir in soya or rice milk to taste and sweeten with honey.

PASTA WITH CREAMY BACON SAUCE

Serves 2

6oz/170g w/f penne pasta or spaghetti
6 rashers of streaky bacon, finely chopped
2 cloves garlic, peeled and crushed
1 carton (250mls) soya cream
2 tablespoons plain soya or goat's yoghurt
salt and pepper to taste
olive oil

Cook the pasta as directed. Meanwhile heat the oil in a heavy based frying pan and add the garlic and bacon and stir quickly for a few minutes, so that they do not burn. Turn down the heat and add the soya cream and season to taste with the salt and pepper. When the pasta is cooked, drain and add to the pan with the bacon sauce and stir through, then add the yoghurt and stir quickly. Serve immediately with a crisp mixed salad.

CINNAMON TOAST

4 slices of any w/f bread
Dairyfree spread
1 tablespoon sugar
1 teaspoon ground cinnamon

Mix together enough Dairyfree spread to cover the bread, with a tablespoon of sugar and a teaspoon of ground cinnamon. Lightly toast the bread on one side, then spread the cinnamon mixture over the uncooked side and toast again until the topping bubbles. (This needs to be done under the grill). Serve hot with a cup of tea!

BREADMAKER BREAD

This recipe works really well in my Panasonic Breadmaker, but adjust it to suit your own breadmaker if the result is not satisfactory.

2 teaspoons of Active Dried Yeast
1½ teaspoons Xanthum Gum
2 teaspoons salt

1 tablespoon sugar
8oz/225g Doves Farm Glutenfree Plain White Flour
7oz/200g buckwheat flakes
400mls hot water
20mls vegetable or olive oil

Put the ingredients into the breadmaker in the order they appear above. Set the breadmaker to Rapid Bake (or the equivalent), as you cannot use the overnight delayed start programme. When the mixing begins, open the lid and, using a plastic spatula, make sure that the flour is well mixed around the edges of the pan. As it is so light in texture it tends not to be well mixed by the machine's paddle. Then close the lid and leave the machine to work its magic. Leave the finished loaf to cool and use as normal bread. The addition of buckwheat flakes gives this bread a better texture and taste.

BISCUITS

4oz/100g soya margarine
40z/100g caster sugar
1 egg, beaten
2oz/50g Gram flour
6oz/175g potato flour
Flavouring eg vanilla essence or zest of lemon or orange
Cook at Gas Mark 4/180C/350F

Beat the soya margarine and sugar together until light and creamy. Beat in the flavouring of choice. Beat in the egg, then add the sifted flours and mix well. As the mixture comes together you may need to use your hands to knead it into a ball. Roll out on a well potato-floured surface and cut into biscuit shapes. Line a baking tray with greaseproof paper or baking parchment and place the biscuits onto it. Cook on the middle shelf for about 20 minutes until a light golden brown. Remove from the oven and place on a wire rack to cool. Store in an airtight tin.

INDEX

Please note: The information about products is believed to be correct at the time of going to press, but neither author nor publisher can accept responsibility for consequences of any inaccuracy found due to unintentional error or subsequent change in product formulation.